Healing
a Broken Heart

*A Guided Journal
Through the Four Seasons
of Relationship Recovery*

A FIRESIDE BOOK

Published by Simon & Schuster

New York   London   Toronto   Sydney   Singapore

Healing
a Broken Heart

Sarah La Saulle, Ph.D.,

and Sharon Kagan, M.F.A., M.A.

FIRESIDE
Rockefeller Center
1230 Avenue of the Americas
New York, NY 10020

FIRESIDE and colophon are registered trademarks
of Simon & Schuster, Inc.

For information about special discounts for bulk purchases,
please contact Simon & Schuster Special Sales:
1-800-456-6798 or business@simonandschuster.com

Designed by Katy Riegel

Manufactured in the United States of America

1   3   5   7   9   10   8   6   4   2

Library of Congress Cataloging-in-Publication Data
La Saulle, Sarah, 1953–
Healing a broken heart : a guided journal through the four seasons
of relationship recovery / Sarah La Saulle and Sharon Kagan.
p.   cm.
1. Man-woman relationships—Miscellanea. 2. Separation (Psychology)—Miscellanea.
3. Grief—Miscellanea. 4. Diaries—Authorship. I. Kagan, Sharon, 1953– II. Title.
HQ801 .L27 2003
306.7—dc21
2002036682

ISBN 978-0-7432-2218-1

Permissions begin on page 233.

To my mother, Honey,

and my daughter, Brooke—

two truly authentic people who share the gift of exquisite empathy.

—SARAH LA SAULLE

To my husband, Terry,

a man with an enormous capacity to love.

For all the meals he cooked while Sarah and I worked at the computer.

And, more important, for being completely devoted

to healing his broken heart.

—SHARON KAGAN

Acknowledgments

THIS BOOK WAS BORN out of the wisdom and courage of many people—those who had the strength to heal their broken hearts and those who saw the value the book would have for others on this path. They are teachers, guides, and healers one and all.

First, we would like to thank our agent, Leslie Daniels, at Joy Harris Literary Agency, for believing in our proposal. Her wholehearted acceptance of our work has continuously encouraged us throughout this lengthy process. She is a perceptive, wise, and gentle person and we are very lucky to have been guided by her. Also, a special thank you to Rhoda Huffey for making this vital introduction.

It is very gratifying that our editor, Lisa Considine, understood and wanted our project for Simon & Schuster. She has fortified us with strong suggestions, important editing, and a necessary comprehension of the depth of this topic. We knew that she was the perfect editor for our book since there was an immediate alignment and grasp of our vision.

It has been an honor and a privilege to know our many patients and students who have valiantly worked at grieving, healing, and taking the risk to love again.

Originally this material was developed as part of a course that Sarah taught at the Esalen Institute. Thanks to Nancy Lunney for selecting this idea for her amazing schedule of classes. The group that assembled for five days worked long and hard on these questions, grieved together, and supported one another. Their work confirmed our belief that this was an approach that others would value.

There have been those gifted people who with their vision, wisdom, strength, and compassion have helped us heal our broken hearts. They are Susan Flynn, Myra Pomerantz, Breck Costin, David Shepard, and Iris Dragin Blum.

Our family and friends are too numerous to list here, although we have the urge to do so. Their generous confidence and ongoing support has been invaluable. We sincerely hope that each of you knows you are in our hearts with gratitude and love.

—S.L. and S.K.

A very warm thank you to Terry Holzgreen for giving Sharon and me the space to accomplish this task, for feeding me extraordinary meals, and for his unqualified approbation.

It is difficult to fully express my thankfulness for Sharon Kagan's participation in my life. My definition of a perfect partner is someone who understands what you are thinking even before you say it, someone who is able to think creatively in all kinds of circumstances, and whose contribution to the task is as relentless as your own, someone who never complains when the hard work becomes overwhelming, but instead finds the humor in it, and, finally, someone whose compatibility with you is so effortless that you no longer can separate your efforts from theirs—Sharon has all of these great qualities, and our commitment to each other has been unparalleled.

—S.L.

Thanks to Terry, a remarkable man; a gifted writer, artist, and woodworker; the king of jiggle therapy; my honey, my lover, my heart, who always wondered why Sarah and I started working on this book right after he and I got engaged.

Sarah, thank you for asking me to work with you on this and every other "hair-brained-idea-for-a-book" that you'll ever have. Can you believe it? It's actually a book. As you know, that's something I never considered a feasible outcome. You've been the perfect partner, always able to work on the parts I was unable to face, crediting me with fixing your writing when all I ever did was type it into the computer. You trusted me implicitly, never losing sight of the importance of the work and yet didn't take the little things too seriously. We've cried together and, more important, laughed together. I love you.

—S.K.

Healing
a Broken Heart

Anecdote

So silent I when Love was by
    He yawned, and turned away;
But Sorrow clings to my apron-strings,
    I have so much to say.

—Dorothy Parker

Introduction

LOSING A LOVER through a breakup or a divorce is one of the most profound and painful experiences of life. This book is specifically designed for anyone who is having difficulty letting go of a romantic relationship. If you are considering ending a relationship, have just recently ended one, or you broke up with a loved one twenty years ago, this guide will facilitate your movement toward resolution.

No matter how much support you have, it can be a terribly lonely time—because of the grief itself but also because it feels as if no one can go through it with you. This guide was created as a companion. It will ask you to consider all the areas of the relationship that you will need to recognize in order to fully let go of it. It will accompany you through the process as intimately as a therapist and a best friend.

The pages that follow are separated, into seasons as a method of dividing different periods of mourning, since grief can be a long, undifferentiated experience.

The four seasons symbolize a complete cycle of grief, each season or stage of grief is a distinct emotional experience.

There is tacit comfort in thinking of the mourning process as having seasons. Human beings understand that one season will definitely follow another, that spring always comes after winter. The guide communicates this idea indirectly, through the specific questions that lead the reader through a particular phase and into the following one.

Of course, the cycle of seasons never truly ends. There is always movement and change. Although we may complete or resolve a current loss, there will be other losses that will once again trigger the full cycle of the mourning process.

This guide encourages you to complete a full, healthy cycle of mourning. The greater purpose in this process is to accept past losses that might otherwise intrude on the life you're trying to live after that loss. If you have not fully grieved a past loss, it will come up again. Paradoxically, when you do give yourself the time you need to grieve, you're left with greater faith in the meaning of life.

One of the amazing things about looking into the past is that it brings to the surface unconscious patterns, belief systems, and old wounds from childhood that you unwittingly may be trying to heal through your current relationships.

We wrote this guide for many reasons. In both our professional and personal lives, we have faced grave heartbreak and loss. Each of us has explored grief and the healing process, the meaning of loss, the purpose of change, and the joy of renewal. The individuals we work with bring their heartbreak to us on a daily basis. We share the quest for answers and learn to live with the questions. For the last twenty years, we have led people to pursue a sense of meaning, to take the risks that have been avoided, to empower their lives in the midst of their deepest pain. We have learned how to create a safe environment for others to do this work in order to recognize their feelings, and authentically express themselves.

Sharon, as an artist and teacher, and Sarah, as a psychotherapist and teacher, understand the importance of process. This is a journey made up of microsteps, incremental shifts that will one day bring you to an entirely new place.

Guidelines

The following questions are organized in a manner that will guide you through a complete cycle of grieving but, that said, there is no right or wrong way to do this work. Some people prefer to dedicate one long weekend to this process, others take several months. If you find that you can't answer one section because it's too difficult, or you can't relate to the questions—don't worry. Allow your heart to lead you onward to another page. Or take a break and pick up the guide again in a few weeks. There is no defined path in the grieving process. Just as we love differently, we grieve differently.

One way to use the guide is to devote twenty minutes a day to answering one or two questions. We suggest that you write during the times when you would ordinarily be lost in your grief. If you are like most people, this is late at night, when you're feeling most alone.

Whether you try to complete *Healing a Broken Heart* over the course of a few days or many months, we ask that you follow these simple guidelines:

- Along with the book, have extra paper prepared. Don't be confined by the space in the book. Write until you are finished.
- Set a timer for ten to twenty minutes. You'll need at least ten minutes to break through any resistance you might have to a particular question, or to the process itself.
- Once you start writing, don't stop, pause, reread, edit, or correct in any way. Just let the words flow.
- Say to yourself, "Keep going, keep going, keep going."
- Don't stop to read what you've already written. You can repeat yourself, write in fragments, isolated words, or whole sentences.

Once ten minutes have passed and you've broken through your initial resistance, you'll discover you have more to say than you ever imagined. If you find yourself in the middle of a thought when the timer goes off, keep writing!

Friends and Professionals

We all have different needs when we face the challenge of overcoming the loss of a love. For some this is, and needs to be, an independent journey. For other people the worst part of grieving is the feeling of isolation. For those of you who feel that you need support in getting through this time, we have several suggestions.

- Find a friend, and schedule times to write together or times to read sections to each other.
- Put a small group together to work through the guide as a group activity. Agree upon guidelines for the meetings. In our workshops we use a timer to limit the writing time, then everyone takes a turn reading. There is no improvising; each member of the group simply reads from the page they've written. If the group agrees, you might allow some time at the end of each meeting to share other feelings. This should be structured time, with a limit on each person's share. If you feel the allotted time wasn't enough to fully address the question, finish your writing at home. Ask someone in the group if they're willing to exchange any additional thoughts with you later.
- If you are working with a therapist, ask your therapist if it would be appropriate for you to share the guide with him/her by reading portions of it as needed. Take your journal to your sessions.

Summer

Summer

"Is it or is it not the end?"

THIS FIRST SEASON is full of vacillation. Whether you have just ended the relationship or it is about to end, at least one of the partners is probably full of doubt. Maybe one of you can't make a commitment, is too controlling, or is simultaneously involved with someone else. Summer's ambivalence and confusion may stem from other roots. Maybe you feel strongly that this relationship won't work out, but you just can't end it. Perhaps you've already ended it, or your partner has left you, but you can't stop thinking about whether it should have ended.

The end of a relationship is complicated by the fact that the coming apart takes place on many levels. There is a physical separation that may include getting your personal belongings back, moving, an absence of daily contact, or a change in your day-to-day activities. Emotionally you are in turmoil, because the reality hasn't sunk in yet. You may imagine you are in the middle of a bad dream, that soon you'll awaken and find everything the way it was. Even if you saw the end coming, it's still a

shock. You might initially feel relief, but this is followed by the uncertainty and pain of letting go.

When you have been "dumped," the experience is intensified and embellished by feelings of anger, betrayal, abandonment, and disappointment. Equivocation and self-doubt color everything.

WE ARE ABOUT to begin a journey together. It is a journey that includes revisiting the good and the bad of the relationship. Along the way you will be asked to examine who you were when the relationship began, what your needs were, and what motivated you to enter into this relationship. This may bring up old wounds, wounds that have been waiting to be healed. We will walk through the feelings together. Before you try any of these exercises, take a moment to quietly settle into a comfortable spot. Take a deep breath, read the following questions, and then write down anything and everything that comes to mind. Don't plan your thoughts; simply share them as if you were telling a dear friend.

What was happening in
your life just prior to
meeting your loved one?
How were you emotionally?
Mentally?

Retrospect

Thanks for
what will be
the memory
if it is.

—Robert Creeley

THE FOLLOWING QUESTIONS bring you back to the beginning of the relationship. Take yourself back to the time when the relationship began. Close your eyes and let your mind fill in the details of that phase of your life. Think about the texture of your life; the questions you asked yourself and the dreams you had.

What were you
working on in your life?
What were your goals?

....

....

....

....

....

....

....

Where and how did
you meet or get together?

....

....

....

....

....

....

What attracted you?
What did you like initially?
Describe him or her.

....

....

....

....

....

....

....

God instructs the heart not by ideas, but by pains and contradictions.

—JEAN PIERRE DE CAUSSADE

AFTER MANY YEARS of being alone, Jackie got involved with a man who turned out to be a poor choice. Many months of pain and struggle led to a breakup, but during that time she learned that she could be in a relationship, and that she would be a good partner with the right man. In the months that followed, she was flooded with prospects, among them her future husband. Though the first relationship was painful and ultimately failed, it was only because of what she had learned there that she was ready and able to commit to a man who was a good mate.

He Said:

He said: I want you to be happy.

He said: I love you so.

Then he was gone.

For two days I was happy.

For two days, he loved me so.

After that, I was on my own.

—Alice Walker

G IVE YOURSELF PERMISSION to go back to the very beginning. Recall the early dates, the telephone conversations, the moment when you knew that you were getting more involved. Allow yourself to remember the feelings of excitement and promise of that time.

What were your hopes,

dreams, and expectations

for this relationship?

....

....

....

....

....

....

....

....

....

....

....

....

....

What were the best

parts of the relationship?

....

....

....

....

....

....

....

....

....

When one is pretending, the entire body revolts.

—ANAÏS NIN

BECAUSE YOU WANTED to love and be loved, you were blind to the parts of your ex that contradicted your positive feelings. Even when the heart says yes, oftentimes the body knows otherwise.

Stephen had scheduled a romantic weekend getaway. There were already significant problems in the relationship; in fact, he knew that there was no real future with his girlfriend. But he wasn't ready to call it quits. He was on his way out to his car when he fell down a few stairs and broke his leg. Later he said he knew it was his body telling him not to go.

LIGHT A CANDLE as a symbol of the clarity you seek. Close your eyes and picture a crystalline, clear pool of water. On the mirrorlike surface of the pool, imagine you see the course of your relationship reflected back to you. Ask to see all the times you were hurt or disappointed, the moments when you began wondering if this relationship was good for you or if you were going to get what you needed from it.

What did you try to
ignore, overlook, or excuse
about this relationship?
What were the worst parts?
Were you feeling disap-
pointed, angry, confused,
hopeless?

THERE WAS A TIME before you knew your partner. Once s/he entered your life, the landscape changed; you met each other's friends and perhaps each other's families. When you end a relationship, the very fabric of your life changes.

How did your
ex-partner fit in with
your circle of friends
and family?

THERE ARE SO MANY CHANGES that come with a breakup. We invest ourselves in our partner's life and family. When you bond with the loved one's family, this can add to the feelings of loss when the relationship ends. Take a moment to remember each of these relationships.

How did you get along
with the important people
in your ex-partner's life?

....
....
....
....

....
....
....
....
....
....

How do you feel about
these people now? Do you feel
that any of these individuals
contributed to the demise of
the relationship? If so, how?

....
....
....
....
....

....
....
....
....
....

The heart that breaks open can contain the whole universe.
—JOANNA ROGERS MACY

THERE IS A PLACE in your heart where you hope to find someone to fulfill deep, unmet needs from childhood. Though that hope is natural and universal, the truth is that these childhood needs can *never* be met. The people who might have fulfilled those needs didn't. Lovers you become involved with may meet needs you have now; they will contribute to your life in other ways, but they can't give you what was missing from your childhood. That was then, this is now. This longing that the heart clings to must be broken and the mourning process for what was lost must commence. Until that occurs, your ability to open your heart, and thus be open to life, is encumbered.

PICTURE YOURSELF in nature, standing beside a rapidly moving river. On the other side of the river is your partner/ex-partner. You can see your former life, but you know that it is no longer meant to be. Imagine the landscape where your partner stands, then the side of the river where you are standing. Then turn your back on your partner and look to the future.

What do you tell
yourself about your
prospects for the future,
knowing that this
relationship won't last
or start again?

THERE IS A DEBATE raging inside you. You might imagine that there are two voices arguing: one argues to keep the relationship alive while the other argues against it. For the next question, you may want to divide your time into two parts. Set a timer for ten minutes and write down everything you love about this relationship. Then reset the timer and write for ten minutes about the things you'll gladly do without. Once you start writing, keep going. Don't worry about spelling or grammar. You might write a list of key phrases rather than sentences. It doesn't matter. Just write and write and write. If you need more time, let yourself have it, but give the "other" side equal time.

What are the thoughts that you weigh against one another? What can't you live with, what can't you live without?

Never try to teach a pig how to sing. It
wastes your time and annoys the pig.
—SOURCE UNKNOWN

W E'VE ALL HEARD from friends about a new partner who would be perfect except for a few vital defects. Their idea is that once the defects are remedied, this will be a good match. You may even have thought that your friend should know better. If she cannot accept her partner as he is, it is best that they both move on. No one is perfect, but that is a far cry from going into a relationship expecting the other person to change.

Years ago Meredith had fallen deeply in love with a married man. He told her that she was like no other. This man was known to have had many affairs during his marriage. She believed that his feelings for her were different, that he would never let her go. They talked about the future; marriage, children. He said he would leave his wife after the holidays, after the opening of a business, after his daughter's graduation. He never left.

Perhaps he never would let her go. As long as she was willing to accept the situation as it was, the relationship endured. So in the end it was she—strengthened by the knowledge that this affair would never be enough for her happiness—who had to end the relationship.

CLOSE YOUR EYES and spend a few moments focusing your attention on your breathing. Imagine that each warming breath takes you deeper and deeper inside. It is time to visit the most authentic part of you, the place referred to as "home." Picture a beautiful spot; it may be somewhere you've been before, it could be in nature, or it could be a place you've seen only in your imagination. You speak the truth here; you hear the small, still voice of your authentic self. Imagine standing before a mirror and looking at your reflection. Now ask to see a true reflection of your relationship, to have your eyes opened. Look into your eyes, deep within, as you examine your conscience.

What do you know will never
change in this relationship? Are
you afraid that what you're
looking for in a relationship
doesn't exist?

....

....

....

....

....

....

....

....

....

....

What do you tell yourself about
the relationship that you follow with
"but . . ." (i.e., "I know he can't make a
commitment, but he loves me." Or:
"She is always criticizing me, but I
think she can change.")?

....

....

....

....

....

....

....

....

....

Life shrinks or expands according to one's courage.

—ANAÏS NIN

IT'S AMAZING HOW often people fight to hold on to things that are not good for them. You fight to hold on to a bad relationship because you are afraid. If you knew that love was out there, it would be easy to move on. It takes courage to act in your own best interest even though you don't know if you will find love again.

Don was in a loveless relationship for ten years. There had been no affection and no sex for many years. For much of that time, he told himself that his partner, Paul, was a decent person, just badly hurt, but finally he knew he could not go on. Don risked being alone for the possibility of finding love. The first sign that a better life was possible appeared at work. After years of just getting by, his business began to prosper. And after a time of mourning, he found love again too.

W HETHER YOU'VE ENDED a relationship or are just considering the possibility, it's a painful time. Together we've examined the many facets of the relationship—the good, the bad, the heartache, and the joy. As you untangle the threadlike attachments, you begin to see that with kindness and thoughtfulness you can make your way free of the loved one.

What part of the relationship is most difficult to let go of?

A Very Short Song

Once, when I was young and true,
Someone left me sad—
Broke my brittle heart in two;
And that is very bad.

Love is for unlucky folk,
Love is but a curse.
Once there was a heart I
     broke;
And that, I think, is worse.

—Dorothy Parker

YOU'VE DONE a tremendous amount of work on the emotional aspect of breaking up; now it's time to look at practical concerns. Remember to be patient with yourself. Take time to write about both the logistics of breaking up and all the feelings that arise as you consider these important details.

What is required for you to actually break up? You may need to separate your belongings, move out, deal with mutual friends. You may have lots of free time to fill, or have to think of ways to avoid the person and the triggers that remind you of the relationship, such as particular songs or places you spent time together.

Summer Ritual

IT'S TIME TO GO inside and speak to the truth teller within. For this process you will need a stack of magazines of all varieties, for example: *National Geographic, Guns & Ammo,* any interior design magazine, fashion magazine, art and photography periodical. Make sure you have a selection of magazines with good photos. Gather up ten to fifteen magazines, a glue stick, and a large piece of paper or poster board. Give yourself permission to tear out anything that catches your eye, whether it's an image, a spot of color, or words or patterns. Things that catch your attention include those that disturb and repulse you, as well as attract you. Don't censor, just tear out anything and everything that stops your eye. If you find yourself thinking about something that you saw long after you've turned the page, go back and get it. Don't start with a theme or look for a theme. Simply collect what captures your imagination. When you can't look any longer, begin to lay out all the images; tear or cut away any extraneous paper. Now you'll begin to notice relationships. Cluster the images that seem connected. Make notes on what you see. If there are pages that no longer interest you, throw them away. Give yourself at least a week to sort, toss, and add images if you'd like. Every day make a different arrangement of the clippings. As you look at each new arrangement, sit down with your journal and ask your inner truth teller what your future holds, or, more specifically, "What is the future of this relationship?" or "What is my future without this relationship?" Write all you see. Follow this procedure each time you rearrange the papers.

When you feel ready to commit to one arrangement, make a collage. This time ask your question before you begin to work on the collage; let your eyes and hands lead the way. Trust your gut. Live with the finished product and listen to the voice within.

Autumn

Autumn

"It's over, and my friends are sick of hearing about it."

YOU KNOW IT'S OVER but you hold on to the hope that this is just a phase to be gotten through. Perhaps you never see your old partner, but you can't stop obsessing about him/her. You feel a great need to talk endlessly about what happened, going over the details in your mind and discussing how you feel. Occasionally, you run into your ex and feel a flush of conflicting emotions—fear, excitement, anger, and desire. While you want to appear to have gotten over him/her, you end up having sex again, only to be left feeling miserable and wanting.

Friends want you to get over this and get on with life. They try to introduce you to new people or encourage you to get out more. But at this point, your primary motivation for social-izing may be to escape this unbearable state in which you find yourself. You fantasize about run-ning into your ex, with your new love. Unfortu-nately, you also picture yourself seeing your ex with someone new. Ouch. The emotions of this season run from numbness to frustration to thwarted desire to hopelessness to rage. Both loss and long-ing are ever present.

Let Evening Come

Let the light of late afternoon
shine through chinks in the barn, moving
up the bales as the sun moves down.

Let the cricket take up chafing
as a woman takes up her needles
and her yarn. Let evening come.

Let dew collect on the hoe abandoned
in long grass. Let the stars appear
and the moon disclose her silver horn.

Let the fox go back to its sandy den.
Let the wind die down. Let the shed
go black inside. Let evening come.

To the bottle in the ditch, to the scoop
in the oats, to air in the lung
let evening come.

Let it come as it will, and don't
be afraid. God does not leave us
comfortless, so let evening come.

—Jane Kenyon

IMAGINE THAT WE are sitting together, settled into a comfy spot; there is nowhere else to go and nothing else to do. We have all the time in the world. I want to hear it all, tell me everything you remember about the actual breakup.

How did it end?

Why?

Who ended it and when?

Western Wind

Western wind, when will thou blow,
    The small rain down can rain?
Christ, that my love were in my
arms
    And I in my bed again!

—Anonymous (Fifteenth century)

CLOSE YOUR EYES and take three deep breaths. With each breath imagine that you are going back in time. When you exhale on the third breath, imagine that you are back to the day when you knew that the relationship had ended. What are the feelings/sensations that you have in your body? Often, something you saw or heard made the loss real to you.

What drove home
the realization that your
loss had occurred and
that it was real?

_____

_____

_____

_____

_____

_____

_____

_____

What were your initial
feelings about the ending?
Shock, disbelief, self-blame,
obsessing over what went
wrong, deep sorrow, fear, a
feeling of death, numbness?

_____

_____

_____

_____

_____

_____

_____

_____

Woman's Lament I

And the last perhaps will not return
and knows me not although I burn.
Ah the trees overhead glowingly
and I feel no one feeling me.

—Rainer Maria Rilke

OVER THE YEARS you must have experienced many losses: in childhood a beloved pet, in your teens a good friend who moved away, being rejected by the college of your dreams, and any other relationships that ended. Remember how you felt on those occasions.

What do you habitually do
when you experience a loss?
How is this experience
different or similar?

AFTER A BREAKUP, there are times when you will be flooded with longing. The problem with yearning is that we don't allow ourselves to sit with the feeling. The mind attaches itself to thoughts and remembrances of what once felt good and forgets about the less than perfect. Try to remember the relationship as a whole as you answer the next two questions.

D o you have trouble
remembering what didn't feel good
in the relationship?
When do you have this trouble?

Felicity of Grief!—even Death being kind

Felicity of Grief!—even Death being kind,

Reminding us how much we dared to love!

There, once, the challenge lay, —like a light glove

Dropped as through carelessness—easy to find

Means and excuse for being somewhat blind

Just at that moment; and why bend above,

Take up, such certain anguish for the mind?

Ah, you who suffer now as I now do,

Seeing, of Life's dimensions, not one left

Save Time—long days somehow to be lived through:

Think—of how great a thing were you bereft

That it should weigh so now! —and that you knew

Always, its awkward contours, and its heft.

—Edna St. Vincent Millay

CLOSE YOUR EYES and imagine a room that is hidden. This may be a secret chamber in the heart of a medieval castle, an attic, or a corner in your childhood home. Imagine this inner dwelling as the place you turn to when you are feeling deep disappointment. Notice the colors of the walls, floor coverings, and furniture. Pay attention to the quality of light inside this room. In the safety of this place, open your heart and answer these questions.

List particularly painful experiences or disappointments with your ex. Write in detail about one or more of these difficult and painful experiences. What did this mean to you at the time? What does it mean now? What was taken away from the relationship at these times?

Put on a piece of music that is soft and comforting. Let the music wash over you, offering you love and support. Imagine that the music is the soothing voice of a compassionate friend. Listen for the words. In the presence of this loving voice, answer the following questions.

Do you think that there is something that might have happened that would have saved the relationship? If you had been different, acted differently? If your partner had only_____?

What is your fantasy about the loved one now?

There is something in the pang of change,

More than the heart can bear,

Unhappiness remembering happiness.

—EURIPIDES

I<small>T'S NOT EASY</small> getting over a broken heart. There are constant reminders of the happiness you once had—the things that your ex-partner gave you, favorite spots where the two of you spent time together. Your heart is full of grief and nothing feels worse than remembering the joy that has been lost.

Even without reminders specific to your relationship, you are surrounded by images of love. Advertisers are constantly selling their products with pictures of happy couples lost in love. You can't avoid seeing couples on the street, walking arm in arm. While you are full of sorrow, you long for those times when you knew happiness. These moments deepen the sense of loss.

DURING THE QUIET TIMES when you are alone, in the wee hours of the night, your mind races with thoughts of what is good about your partner/ex-partner. Close your eyes and think about how the relationship lives inside your mind, heart, and body. Imagine that as you write about the relationship you empty yourself of all these thoughts and feelings. Let them live instead on the pages of your journal. Write down everything that comes to mind. Don't hold back, rewrite, or edit in any way—just let the words flow onto the page. Write until you are empty.

Do you harbor secret hopes that someday you'll be together again? What are your fantasies about how this will come to be?

Are you still having contact with the loved one? What is the nature of it? How do you feel after spending time either talking or visiting with each other?

It is hard to know what to say to a person who has been struck by tragedy, but it is easier to know what not to say. Anything critical of the mourner (don't take it so hard, try to hold back your tears, you're upsetting people) is wrong. Anything which tries to minimize the mourner's pain (it's probably for the best, it could be a lot worse, you're better off now) is likely to be misguided and unappreciated. Anything which asks the mourner to disguise or reject his feelings (we have no right to question God. God must love you to have selected you for this burden) is wrong as well.

—HAROLD S. KUSHNER

IF YOU'VE EVER EXPERIENCED a terrible loss, and anyone, out of ignorance, tried to say something to encourage you to get over your feelings, you know that Harold Kushner is right. Remember that your feelings are valid. In fact, part of the healing process is recognizing your feelings and expressing them.

Inside your heart there is a vault filled with words that have never been spoken and feelings that are unexpressed. Look inside and find that place. It may feel like a box or a vault or some other vessel. Open it up and let a purifying breeze blow through it. Take a few deep breaths. As the air stirs the words and feelings, set your timer and write.

The following questions have to do with the people around you and whether or not you feel their concern and support.

What are people saying
to you about your loss?

....

....

....

....

....

....

....

....

....

....

What hurts you about
people's reactions to your
grief? What do others do that
helps you handle your loss?

....

....

....

....

....

....

....

....

....

....

Autumn Project

MAKE A LIST of major and minor losses throughout your life. Start with birth and work your way forward. List anything and everything that crosses your mind. Put a star (*) next to the entries you think of as primary losses. These fundamental losses—such as a parent's death—have affected your entire life, self-concept, and relationships. Circle the losses that you think are still affecting you.

Now make a time line for your life. On one side of the line mark your age and each of the losses on your list (above). On the other side of the line, note the effects the loss had on your life, your personality, or your worldview. Also list any lessons you learned as a result of the experience.

Winter

After great pain, a formal feeling comes—
The Nerves sit ceremonious, like Tombs—
The stiff Heart questions was it He, that bore,
And Yesterday, or Centuries before?

The Feet, mechanical, go round—
Of Ground, or Air, or Ought—
A wooden way
Regardless grown,
A Quartz contentment, like a stone—

This is the Hour of Lead—
Remember, if outlived,
As Freezing persons, recollect the Snow—
First—Chill—then Stupor—then the letting go—

—Emily Dickinson

Winter

"The dark night of the soul."

WINTER IS THE TIME of grief, when all goes black. There is no light, no sound, no direction, no purpose. It's as if all the other days of loss were leading to this full and complete realization. There is no going back. In the previous seasons, hope lived and infiltrated days and nights, lifting the spirits with the fragile longing that your lover might return.

In this season of grief, you realize that not only is your lover not returning, but that he/she may be with another. Obsessive thoughts and images of your replacement are torturing you. He has found someone new. You believe you will be alone forever.

How could anyone ever understand the gravity of this love and the depth of the loss? Might as well turn down that invitation for coffee and stay home. You try to take care of yourself because it seems that no one else will.

Are these ailments, aches, pains, and colds real or imagined? This broken heart breaks the body as well. It is not enough to be plagued by pain in the chest, but now the whole body is racked with pain and feels poorly. It is no longer important to your lost loved one how you are, where you are, or even who you are, and you know this in the bottom of your soul.

If only you could stop blaming yourself, but somehow you believe this is all because of something lacking and miserable about you. That is why nobody can rescue you, nothing will help you now. You've already exposed the worst part of yourself to the only one who mattered. Nothing else could feel this way save death. Though you may not be aware of progress, these feelings tell you that you have come to the heart of winter, the most difficult season of grief.

In this dark season, we'll encourage you to write letters in addition to journal entries, which can be a significant part of the healing process. In writing letters to yourself and your ex, as well as writing letters from various individuals to yourself, unspoken communications become clarified.

You often do not realize the need to say certain things until the moment you sit down to write. Likewise, the letters you write to yourself from others may express feelings that others do not have the capacity to tell you directly. Again, they may not even know what they need to say or should say to help you through this—but you know.

Writing these letters will help you heal residual feelings. There will no longer be words you need to hear or say; everything will be fully expressed.

We believe that by writing these letters, the communication will actually be received on an unconscious level by those you are writing to, and that by spending time with these feelings you will eventually make your own peace with the loss and find the strength to then move on.

PREPARE A PEACEFUL and nurturing environment where you feel safe and will be undisturbed. Perhaps you have a special chair you like to curl up in. Create a soothing ambience using candles, in a soft, comforting place. Be gentle with yourself. Even if you think you have very little to say, give yourself a full fifteen minutes to write. Don't worry about whether or not your writing is a direct response to the question. As you write, give yourself permission to say it all. Write down anything that pops into your mind, no matter what.

Have you ever seen
your ex with someone else?

Is he/she dating now?
With a new partner? Engaged? Married?
Was this a prior relationship?
Are there any stories you know about
this new relationship or the events
surrounding the new partner?

Jealousy is always born together with love, but it does not always die when love dies.

—François, Duc de la Rochefoucauld

You may not consider yourself "the jealous type," but seeing your ex with another causes a special kind of pain. Even if you were the one who chose to end the relationship, it is still discomfiting to think of your ex-lover with another. The sensations of possession and familiarity are often very strong for quite a while after a breakup.

Many years ago, I ended a relationship with a man I knew I did not love. We had been together for several years and I found it hard to break up with him because he was such a kind person. Months later he met a woman who moved in with him while I had yet to begin dating again. The level of jealousy and pain I felt surprised me.

You've set aside time to be with this guide, now give yourself permission to tell this trusted companion the truth about what you are feeling. It's okay, you're completely safe—you can say everything you've been holding inside. This may be the one place where you can speak freely. Go ahead and write, letting the pen lead the way. You don't have to know what you're going to say ahead of time, rather, trust the words to flow out of your heart and onto the paper.

How do you feel about your ex's current social/marital status?

Do you have any recurring thoughts about your ex's new partner or their relationship? What are they?

YOUR HEART IS broken. No one really seems to understand the anguish that you feel. You may be worried that you're exhausting your friends' patience when you talk about how you're feeling. There are thoughts you can't bear to admit to anyone, thoughts about your ex loving someone else. You have all the time you need; there is no need to edit. This guide can hear it all, even the most embarrassing thoughts or wildest fantasies.

W hat are your fantasies
about the ex-partner's
relationship and future?

_____

_____

_____

_____

_____

_____

_____

_____

_____

_____

_____

_____

_____

_____

_____

_____

Tonight I Can Write

Tonight I can write the saddest lines.

Write, for example, "The night is starry
and the stars are blue and shiver in the distance."

The night wind revolves in the sky and sings.

Tonight I can write the saddest lines.
I loved her, and sometimes she loved me too.

Through nights like this one I held her in my arms.
I kissed her again and again under the endless sky.

She loved me, sometimes I loved her too.
How could one not have loved her great still eyes.

Tonight I can write the saddest lines.
To think that I do not have her. To feel that I have lost her.

To hear the immense night, still more immense without her.
And the verse falls to the soul like dew to the pasture.
What does it matter that my love could not keep her.
The night is starry and she is not with me.

This is all. In the distance someone is singing. In the distance.
My soul is not satisfied that it has lost her.

My sight tries to find her as though to bring her closer.
My heart looks for her, and she is not with me.

The same night whitening the same trees.
We, of that time, are no longer the same.

I no longer love her, that's certain, but how I loved her.
My voice tried to find the wind to touch her hearing.

Another's. She will be another's. As she was before my kisses.
Her voice, her bright body. Her infinite eyes.

I no longer love her, that's certain, but maybe I love her.
Love is so short, forgetting is so long.

Because through nights like this one I held her in my arms
my soul is not satisfied that it has lost her.
Though this be the last pain that she makes me suffer
and these the last verses that I write for her.

—Pablo Neruda

YOU ARE IN the deepest phase of your grief, the dark night of the soul. Be gentle with yourself. These are the days when this guide can offer you the most comfort. Trust this process—give yourself to it. If memories of other relationships come to the surface, write about those too.

Do you have any
impulses relating to the
partner's new love interest?
What are they?

....

....

....

....

....

....

....

....

....

....

....

Does your ex want you to be
friends with the new partner?
How are you handling this?

....

....

....

....

....

....

....

....

Doing This

I'm driving back and forth
on the gravel lane
before the two-room, stucco house

of the woman I love. She's inside,
making love with a woman
whose white car is parked in the driveway

and it, this car, disturbs me
more than anything. It sticks out of itself
so far into my life. Each time I pass,

I know, with a ten-pound sadness in my chest,
that I can't keep doing this.
And now I realize, far too late,

I should have fought for her, should have
wept and begged and made the full,
hair-extracting spectacle

of what I felt. I should have
shed my pride.
What good is pride? When you die,

I know they turn you
inside out, to see what portion
of your god-alloted guts

you failed to spend on earth.
The ones who arrive in heaven
without a kopek of their fortune left

are welcomed, cheered, embraced.
The rest are chastised and reborn
as salesmen and librarians.

It's so simple,
and that's what gets me—that every time
I drive up and down this street,

looking at that white Toyota in the drive,
it messes up not just this life,
but my eternity as well.

But I keep doing it,
dragging myself back and forth
over this corner of the world

which scrapes and grinds against me,
like a rock on the bow of a ship.
Etching the errors in my surface

deeper, and deeper. And less forgiven.

—Tony Hoagland

W E SUGGEST THAT you begin working on these questions in front of a full-length mirror. Look yourself in the eye. We rarely take the time to look at ourselves. Pay attention to the things you tell yourself about who you are and how you look. This very simple act of looking at yourself is likely to stir up deep feelings. Take five minutes to just look at yourself. Either silently or out loud, ask yourself the following questions. Then go to your special spot. It may be in bed under the covers, or in a big overstuffed chair. It's the spot you always return to when you want to have a heart-to-heart with yourself. Write as fast as you can, so that you can't possibly hesitate or hold back.

Do you compare yourself to your ex's new partner? If you've never seen this person, what comparisons do you imagine?

....

....

....

....

....

....

....

....

....

....

What bad feelings do these comparisons cause? Any good ones?

....

....

....

....

....

....

....

....

WORKING ON THESE questions in front of a full-length mirror, it is useful to know what you say to yourself about your appearance. Take five minutes to just gaze at yourself. Either silently or out loud, ask yourself the following questions; phrase them in the first person.

Do you have any
negative thoughts about
your future? Your age?
Your attractiveness?

....

....

....

....

....

Do you feel messages
from the culture regarding
your age, future, and
attractiveness?

....

....

....

....

....

....

....

....

....

....

Your Soul Shines

Your soul shines
like the sides of a fish.
My tears are salty
my grief is deep.
Come live in me again.
Each day I walk along the edges
of the tall rocks.

—Alice Walker

CLOSE YOUR EYES and allow yourself to drift inside to a cozy corner of your inner world. This is the one special place where you are always safe. Imagine that you make your way to this secret world; it may be a garden, a peaceful room, or a sanctuary that you've visited before. A special friend meets you there; it may be an animal guide or someone who loves you. You hear him/her call your name and just the sound of his/her voice makes you feel protected. It is time to share your thoughts and feelings with this loving presence. When you are ready to open your heart and mind, open your eyes and write down everything.

Are you blaming yourself—for what?

A Song

Now I am calm. It seems that nothing
can make me feel the same exhausting pain.

What is another's harrowing to me?
Grief is not a lake,

I am miles at sea, miles
from the moving figures—

Why are they calling out?
They cluster at land's edge as though

the stony promontory,
where they had just been standing,

were sheared away.
If they are frightened,

if they also grieve,
let them comfort one another,

I cannot help them, I am riding
each enormous wave of this absence
that knows no further shore.

—Ellen Bryant Voigt

POUR YOURSELF a cup of tea. Imagine that you are sitting with a gentle witness. It is in the company of this welcome presence that you can say the unthinkable. This presence may come to you as the image of a cat curled up beside you, as a force in nature, or as someone who you know loves you completely.

Are you around friends whose circumstances seem better than yours—what sort of impact does this have on you? The friendship?

YOU ARE NOW ready to address the one you loved, your friends, and your family in letters. Give yourself a minimum of thirty minutes to write without stopping, pausing, editing, or correcting spelling or grammar. Keep going, keep going, keep going.

Write a letter to the loved one about the ending—include what happened, how you felt, what you already said, what you never said.

IMAGINE SCRIBING a magic circle around you. The circle is filled with beautiful-colored light. When you are inside the circle, you are empowered to say and feel anything that has been kept secreted away inside your heart. This may be a feeling that you haven't dared admit to yourself. Imagine that your ex is seated at a distance, opposite you, and s/he is also surrounded by a circle of light. It is time to unburden yourself.

Write a letter to the loved one about what you wanted, what you were hoping and longing for, what your dreams were, what you feel you don't want to give up on.

CLOSE YOUR EYES and visualize a place that is rich and deep. It might be a study with an overstuffed chair, or a library decorated in the beautiful tones of aged oak bookshelves. In this room there is an enormous book; it sits open on top of a large table. You walk over to the book to see what it is about and there at the top of the page is your name. On one side of the page you see all of your accomplishments; on the other side of the page are the memories that comprise your regrets, errors, and lessons that were hard learned.

Write about anything that you blame yourself for—regrets, mistakes in judgment, embarrassments, lessons, things you'd like to do over again, things you'd never do again.

It isn't for the moment you are stuck that you need courage, but for the long uphill climb back to sanity and faith and security.

—ANNE MORROW LINDBERGH

IN THE DEPTH of grief, it feels like injury is piled upon injury. You may remember people who were less than supportive of the relationship, people who had ill wishes for you or your partner.

In college my boyfriend had a best friend, someone I never trusted. My boyfriend had been in love with her throughout high school, and he claimed they were just friends. But when she called, he ran.

We had important plans for an upcoming family event. The friend asked him to help her move out of town. I knew he'd never make it back in time, but he swore he would. I later learned that she'd planned all along on his being with her for three days, but only told him after they were on the road. I was as angry with her as I was with him.

First there was the loss itself, but loss is generally complicated. Not only did I have to let go of the boyfriend, but I had to overcome the sense of betrayal and deep disappointment I felt.

PICTURE YOURSELF someplace in nature, where you are surrounded by beauty. Close your eyes and turn within. Where are your thoughts? How does your body feel? What is the state of your heart? Look inside to the ledger in your heart. On this list you will find the names of those people who have been involved in any way with this breakup, people who have hurt you knowingly or unknowingly. With each breath you take, your heart lightens and the list becomes clear. Sit here quietly for a few minutes and let the names float onto the list. When you know all the names, open your eyes.

Are there individuals associated with the ending who have hurt you? If so, write each of them a letter (long or brief) telling them exactly what you think and feel about them.

IMAGINE THAT a magic bubble protects you; nothing can harm you or intrude on you. Knowing that you are safe and that you can speak freely, imagine that you run into your ex's new partner or future partner. Pay attention to your body, including feelings of pain or discomfort. It's okay; you can feel all the feelings and say anything you want.

W rite a letter to the loved one's new partner telling them anything you would like to about your feelings toward him/her, your relationship with your ex, any thoughts or feelings, such as a warning about your ex-partner. If you could put any information about your ex on the Internet, what would it be?

THE TIME HAS come to clear your heart. Turn to your trusted guide and give voice to your anger. These can be the most difficult things to say, write, or even think. Give yourself permission. Sometimes it helps to dance wildly or beat on your chest. It's okay, no one is watching. Remember all those times your ex hurt or disappointed you. Here is your opportunity to clear the air and give your heart a chance to move on. Set your timer for thirty minutes and don't hold back, write it all out. No one will ever see this letter—it's only for you.

Write an angry letter to the loved one and let it all out—complain, be furious, mean and nasty, disappointed. Say absolutely anything that you want to about him or her in this letter.

'Tis better to have loved and lost than never to have loved at all.

—ALFRED, LORD TENNYSON

WHEN YOU WERE a child, you probably had a crush on a schoolmate. Perhaps you liked her and she didn't like you back. People think that first love is "cute" and call it a crush. But if you remember it well, you'll remember that it was painful.

A lucky child has parents who are sensitive to these experiences and have created an open and communicative environment where he can talk about his feelings. It is an unusual situation for a child to have a parent who is supportive and nurturing about early love losses—but it is the best time to begin to learn that we can suffer a loss, feel the pain, and then grow from it.

Robert had parents who were deeply wounded. As is often the case with children of Holocaust survivors or survivors of other major traumas, his parents could not tolerate his sorrow. Their response to him—at times spoken, at other times implied—was, "This isn't pain, I know what real pain feels like."

The result was that he didn't learn to honor his feelings. The message he heard loudly and clearly from his parents was that compared to their "real" feelings, his were insignificant. Not only did this leave him ignorant about how one might deal with a loss, he avoided intimate relationships and any resulting feelings altogether.

YOU'VE BEEN WORKING so hard. These letters may not be easy for you, so congratulate yourself. It's time to hear words of love and support. Imagine that your parents are able to be with you exactly as you would want them to be, that they are able to say exactly what you need to hear. If this is impossible for you, then call on the fantasy of good parents inside you. Curl up in your favorite spot and write out all the words your heart aches to hear—acknowledgments, compassionate reflections on what you've gone through in this breakup, and words of encouragement. Go ahead, gush over yourself.

Write a letter to yourself from each of your parents about the loss you are going through now. Make it a letter that expresses their deepest feelings and most positive attitudes toward you and your life.

Sense of Something Coming

I am like a flag in the center of open space.

I sense ahead the wind which is coming, and must live it through.

While the things of the world still do not move:

the doors still close softly, and the chimneys are full of silence,

the windows do not rattle yet, and the dust still lies down.

I already know the storm, and I am troubled as the sea.

I leap out, and fall back,

and throw myself out, and am absolutely alone

in the great storm.

—Rainer Maria Rilke

WE RARELY HEAR the things we need to hear from an ex. Saying good-bye and being set free are vital steps in reaching closure. Close your eyes and visualize your ex-partner standing before you. Ask the best part of him/her to respond to you. Tell him/her what you need in order to move on. Give yourself the gift of good-bye.

Have the loved one
write a good-bye letter to
you saying everything you
need to hear.

Y OU'VE EXPRESSED YOUR anger and hurt. The next step in letting go is acknowledging what was good about your relationship. This is not meant to reawaken the sense of loss. Give yourself credit for the important things you've learned. Assimilate the good that came to you because of the relationship. Acknowledge yourself.

W rite to the ex-partner saying anything that you were grateful for, appreciated in them or that the relationship brought out in you, lessons you learned, and experiences that you wouldn't have wanted to miss.

LIGHT A SCENTED CANDLE, a reminder that this is sacred time. You've gone through so much, revisiting every aspect of this relationship. Close your eyes and take three deep breaths. Imagine that your whole body is filled with compassion. Each inhalation washes through you, bringing a deeper sense of peace and serenity. With each exhalation wash away any lingering feelings of self-doubt.

Write yourself a compassionate, sympathetic letter about what you have learned and understood, what you are grateful to yourself for, what you were courageous about, and what you forgive yourself for.

There is no coming to heaven with dry eyes.

—THOMAS FULLER

THE CAPACITY TO mourn and then recover is one of the greatest gifts you've been given. When you lose a loved one, you don't quite know how you'll ever get over it and yet you will if you can allow yourself to grieve.

Grieving is the process during which you let go of all that you thought you were and would be through your association with your ex. You cry over what you had, what you were going to become, all the things you had yet to do together, and the special times you shared.

Allison gave me detailed descriptions of her new boyfriend's avid courtship. It seemed very promising; they were well suited to each other and shared many hours of laughter. They spoke to each other daily and dated exclusively, in a passionate thrall.

After six months, he suddenly pulled away and became disinterested. Allison was shocked and angry. Her grief had to encompass letting go of the fantasy of the committed, stable relationship that this one would never become. By mourning, she was able to move on and eventually date a man who wanted to be with her beyond the first few months of romance.

You Ask About Madness

A wrong door is opened
by accident.
You enter the vat kingdom.
It is waveless and deep
as a poisoned well.

Asbestos will not save you,
diligence or vaccinations.
Night is a tunnel
for your fist.
The sky disappears.
You hear the pin pulled
on the hand grenade
in your head.

Your legs poise at the oily
waste ink black high tide,
the full count,
the last unspeakable edge
when sleepless and exhausted
you hate each garden
fence slat,
each black blade of grass.

You sense a crowd of scales,
amphibian breaths

and a persistent chill.
Night callouses,

glacial in impact
and you are sheeted,
a pond under ice where rocks
are tossed and lost stars fall
jaded and degenerate,
burning to death.

Sleep brings no deliverance.
Your dreams are small zoos.

You fear the drain of morning,
affliction of sparrows and sun.
You repeat your sins, one by one.
The black dog rears

and breaks his slender chain.
The bloodless slain return
on their accord.

Survival is absolutely random.

—Kate Braverman

Let your compassionate guide receive your experience of grief. Pour your heart out. Take a moment and close your eyes; go inside and listen to your heart.

What has your life been like during the aftermath of this relationship, during this mourning process?

IMAGINE THAT YOU are seated beside a beautiful clear pool of water. Gaze into the water and notice its color and clarity. Does the light dance on the surface of the pool or can you see deep into the water? Ask yourself the following question and watch the answer drift to the surface of your mind.

During this time of heavy

grieving, are there regrets

that are plaguing you?

It's Possible I Am Pushing Through Solid Rock

It's possible I am pushing through solid rock
in flintlike layers, as the ore lies, alone;
I am such a long way in I see no way through,
and no space: everything is close to my face,
and everything close to my face is stone.

I don't have much knowledge yet in grief—
so this massive darkness makes me small.
You be the master: make yourself fierce, break in:
then your great transforming will happen to me,
and my great grief cry will happen to you.

—Rainer Maria Rilke

BURIED MEMORIES REMAIN in your heart, brain, and every cell of your body. Find a place where you can relax. Quiet your mind and focus on your breath as you begin to slow down and relax. Invite unspoken words to drift into your consciousness.

W hat are some of the
words or statements you
would have wanted to
express to others during
several of the past losses
you experienced? What do
you need to say now?

Iᴛ's ᴛɪᴍᴇ ᴛᴏ ʀᴇᴀᴄʜ out to others. Every one of us has a story to tell. Think of someone you know who has suffered a terrible loss. Let them be your guide today. When you remember what happened to them, reflect on what you learned from their experience. Let others help you with your grief.

Write about anyone you know who has survived a terrible loss. What was their loss, how did they get through it, where are they with it now? Interview them for more information.

Good as It Gets

This fall I am content
with the small.
Are you surprised?

I don't beg my married lover
to stay, unpack, commit
his inviolate unformed self
to this raw persona,
this female intelligence
that terrifies.

Just say my mouth tastes
like Hawaiian flowers.
And yes, come and go.
Pass through.
I'm a hotel.

The street is skeletal
at midnight in rain.
Lawns are empty.
Roses plucked and stuck
back in a trunk,
gaudy and spoiled
as the red feather boas

hanging from brass lamps
in the rooms of whores.

I am thirty years old.
I have broken my heart
often and with precision.
It is enough to have silence
at 2 a.m. and Baudelaire
and no one I love rehearsing
suicide or curled up mute
and dying.

It's been weeks without funerals,
asylum Sundays, emergency rooms,
police or bad reviews.
Sirens squeal in the distant west.
I pour another drink, toast
the catatonic wall and kid,
this is as good as it gets.

—Kate Braverman

Spontaneously answer each of the following questions with a quick list. You can write one list at a time or jump back and forth from guilt to sadness to hurt and so forth.

W̲hat are you afraid of? Guilty about? Resentful and angry about? Sad about? Envious and/or jealous of? Hurt by? Regretting?

YOU'VE EXPLORED the emotional pain you've endured; now it's time to write about the ways you've suffered physically. Close your eyes and turn your attention to your breathing. Let your breath be your guide into your body. Slowly scan the length of your body. Start with your toes and work your way up into your legs, to your pelvis, torso, back, shoulders, arms, up into your neck and in your head. Listen to the wisdom of your body and how it has suffered during this time of grief. Give it a voice. Describe your body's journey.

What are the physical symptoms of your loss? Sleeplessness, wanting to sleep all the time, aches and pains, drinking and eating too much, loss of appetite?

Résumé

Razors pain you;

Rivers are damp;

Acids stain you;

And drugs cause cramp.

Guns aren't lawful;

Nooses give;

Gas smells awful;

You might as well live.

—Dorothy Parker

IF YOU'VE BEEN neglecting yourself, the following questions may be difficult to answer. Writing in your journal, working through your grief, is one way you've been good to yourself. If you have the time, answer the questions in one sitting. These questions will help you to focus your attention on self-care.

W hat self-care activities
are difficult for you right
now? What might you
commit to doing every week
that is just for you?

For Women Abandoned in December

They always leave at Christmas.
The poor amnesiacs snap awake
to blood relatives and apple pie.
They join the crusades.
They go to the moon.

You cannot hold them
with your grandmother's lullabies.
Or stories of Harlem whorehouses
you hid in at thirteen,
how they washed your head
of lice, gave you lemonade
and cab fare.

He is packing.
You offer him your childhood
gold locket,
the caftan you knitted
and love letters lavender scented.

He stands at the door.
(He remembers his address!)
You beg him to take more,
the Boston ferns in the hallway,

the kittens, a cashmere scarf,
your passport and bank account.

His eyes are blue
as the flames on kitchen stoves
in cold rooms where you lived
alone at nineteen and winter
yawned skeletal, ghosted
and darkness opened
queer and incalculable.

The door closes
and you are that woman again
abandoned in December
on a night when the sky
is calm and abundant with stars,
more stars than you could harvest.

Night rakes your face.
The 'phone doesn't ring.
The ballerina spinning porcelain
on a music box stops.
The music stops.

—Kate Braverman

TURN OFF the ringer on your phone. Set the stage for some quiet time to reflect on your life. Bring flowers home and place them where you will see them while you write.

What are your
spiritual/philosophical/religious
views on loss? Does it help or
sadden you to think from these
perspectives?

I Live My Life in Growing Orbits

I live my life in growing orbits
which move out over the things of the world.
Perhaps I can never achieve the last,
but that will be my attempt.

I am circling around God, around the ancient tower,
and I have been circling for a thousand years,
and I still don't know if I am a falcon, or a storm,
or a great song.

—Rainer Maria Rilke

Throughout your grief, you've probably experienced better days and worse days. It is especially painful when the rest of the world seems to be celebrating their love—Valentine's Day, birthdays, or big family gatherings. It is important to plan ahead and be particularly kind to yourself. Your writing session today is centered on taking care of yourself by preparing for the difficult days.

What activities and self-protective acts will you plan to help you get through the holidays and any significant anniversary dates connected with the loved one?

This could but have happened once—
And we missed it, lost it forever.
—ROBERT BROWNING

INTIMATE RELATIONSHIPS ARE full of longing for what you never had in childhood. If you could only get the "absent" father to spend time with you, the critical mother to speak kindly, the alcoholic parents to work out their disagreements in a more civilized fashion . . . Unconsciously, you will select partners who will bring up these old longings and you will hope that somehow this new love will be different—kind, communicative, and present. Bruce grew up with a very cruel, envious, critical mother. He chose a woman to marry who seemed very different. His wife seemed lighthearted, easygoing, almost "ditzy." But this wife could never fulfill his old longing for a kind mother. She barely acknowledged him in a loving manner, not because she was cruel, but because she wasn't present enough to notice her husband and love him in the way he had always wanted. This marriage eventually came apart because he needed to mourn his lost mother's love—to fully grieve over it. There it was all along, living in the midst of his marriage.

Winter Ritual

Throughout history, tribal cultures have used ritual to mark the stages of a person's life, giving the initiate a context in which to view ordeals and celebrations. Tribal children witnessed rituals, which created an understanding of life's ups and downs. Ritual is a way to share life's burdens with your community/support system. Most important, ritual serves to open one door and close another. It is a formalized series of actions that state your willingness to change.

The Death

Don't expect to do the following ritual all at once; it is natural for it to happen in stages. Give yourself time to feel your feelings every step of the way.

- Choose a picture of your former partner. Imagine that you are preparing to bury what's dead.
- Gather objects, gifts from the person, that carry a great emotional charge. If you're up to

it, include things you thought you would never part with. These items represent the course of the relationship.

- Put everything in a box.
- Write an obituary for the relationship.
- Write a eulogy to read at the funeral.
- Set the date, time, and place for the funeral.
- Invite friends to come and support you in your time of loss. If you are uncomfortable with other people participating or if this isn't possible, imagine yourself surrounded by loved ones.
- On the appointed day, with friends at your side, dig the hole, put the box of items/the relationship in the hole, and bury it. Say your eulogy and recite poems or prayers that speak to your grief. Invite your friends to speak about the relationship.

When you return home, create a spot that expresses your feelings of loss and emptiness. You may place empty bowls, empty picture frames in this area. Look for items that speak to you about how you feel at this time. Give yourself a week to be with the emptiness. After a week's time, clear this emptiness altar and replace the items with objects and images you love.

Spring

Spring

"The Return to Life"

T HE HEAVINESS OF winter is finally lifting. The excruciating agony of full-out grief has turned into a dull ache. There are minutes, hours, and even days when it doesn't hurt at all. This feels strange, as if something familiar is missing. Emptiness is replaced by the urge to get out, do something, be with someone. Instead of fantasizing about being loved again, you're actually going out and trying to meet new people.

Simple self-care tasks are becoming routine. You return phone calls, do the laundry, wash your hair, exercise—all the things you used to do. Coming back to life is experiencing your body as a helpful, not hurtful, resource.

Now the world seems to be a place full of possibilities—new activities, renewed friendships, and even love.

The passage through this intense cycle of loss and letting go has changed you because you have been willing to honor and express your heart-felt/honest feelings on these pages. Your vulnerability and renewed strength are gifts that you will bring into your next relationship.

Go slowly, letting your whole being awaken.

Think of dating as a way to explore new relationships and be honest about their nature. There is plenty of time to get to know yourself and your deepest needs and enough time to find someone who can truly be a partner to you. Use what you write in response to the first few prompts in this section to make more discerning choices in future relationships.

Every now and then, the painful feelings of loss will resurface. Come to expect this, because life is a continuous process of change, and, ultimately, letting go.

Repetition Compulsion

Repetition compulsion is the unconscious need to re-create an old dynamic/wound in a new relationship in an attempt to achieve a different and healing outcome. Unfortunately, our tendency is to re-create repeatedly the same exact wounding experience.

For example, Rita, the child of an alcoholic, was very careful in her selection of a mate. She picked a boyfriend who showed no interest in drinking during their courtship. Around the time of their marriage, he enjoyed a few nights of raucous drinking. His dalliance with alcohol didn't end with their marriage, in fact, drinking became a habit and then something more. After a few years of marriage, she realized she had married an alcoholic. "How can this be?" she wondered. She swears she didn't see it coming. And yet, there's a certain kind of invisible magnetism between this child of an alcoholic and an alcoholic mate. The problem with recognizing one's repetition compulsion is that the process is an unconscious one. This search to fulfill childhood needs is like trying to get a good, clear view of the back of one's own head.

No matter how many mirrors you look in, the view is still somewhat distorted. Often, we need someone's help (perhaps a therapist's) to look there and tell us what we cannot see.

One aspect of the therapeutic process is to examine one's history for possible themes, patterns, and injuries. What once happened to us is not as important as recognizing how our lives are still being governed by these experiences. We will never know exactly what happened to us, we can only attempt to grasp the meaning we gave it, the feelings that are still caught up in the past, and the way our lives continue to tell the story of our old wounds.

As you respond to the prompts that immediately follow, notice the feelings that surface and write them down. Healing the repetition compulsion comes from the conscious recognition of where we felt wounded, what the feelings are, and directly grieving over the old loss. We cannot change what happened once, long ago; we can only grieve and acknowledge the pain. By actively mourning, the feelings appropriate to the past return to where they belong. We no longer carry them with us, re-creating old, repetitive scenarios in which we long for a way to heal.

We Are Not to Know Why

We are not to know why
this and that masters us;
real life makes no reply,
only that it enraptures us
makes us familiar with it.

—Rainer Maria Rilke

For these next questions, take a moment and recall specific examples of loss that occurred in your family. Give yourself permission to reenter these memories; let the feelings come back. You may find clues in your body. Picture the house in which you grew up, especially a specific room that reminds you of the loss.

Describe a significant family loss and how everyone in your immediate family handled it. What did this mean to you as a child and what does this mean to you as an adult? Be sure to include any feelings that might be surfacing while writing about this loss.

For the most part, everything we've learned about grieving we learned from our families. Just because we have funerals doesn't mean that we grieve well or completely. Many people do not know how to be with a loss, what to say to the mourner, or how to heal.

In general, what did you learn from your family about handling loss and sorrow? What did your parents say or do when someone was ill or died? Did the family discuss loss, feelings, difficult times?

Nothing has a stronger influence psychologically on their environment, and especially on their children, than the unlived life of the parents.

— CARL JUNG

UNMET NEEDS LEFT over from childhood are carried into adult life. When your parents met, they were unconsciously drawn together in an effort to gain the lost love and nurturing that they never received from their parents. No matter how hard they try to be excellent parents, there is still a deep well of childhood losses that influence their adult lives. Your parents and their relationship have been influencing you in great and subtle ways even now, although you may not be aware of it.

A fellow art student, Cheryl, demonstrated great artistic talent, but her family was adamant that her art be relegated to hobby status. When we met she was on her way to becoming an accountant, "something practical."

I learned that her father had also shown great artistic talent. But her grandfather, a renowned painter, had always been too busy to spend any time with his family. In fact, when Grandfather worked he became rageful if he was interrupted. As a result, my friend's father decided that he would never treat his family the way he'd been treated and vowed to keep his art a hobby. He spoke disdainfully of artists and their lives. His opinion had been influencing her for years, even though in her heart of hearts she wanted to pursue this life.

CLOSE YOUR EYES and imagine that every breath you take carries you back in time until you return to the day you were born. Think about the details of your family's circumstances, the place you lived, anyone who lived in the house with you. Envision the stories you were told about your birth. Now picture yourself in elementary school; think about coming home after school. Allow your mind to skip through the years. You're now an adolescent; see your father entering the house after work. Imagine sitting at the dinner table. See your parents sharing time together and try to remember the details. Recall a time when your parents had a fight. Think of a family vacation. Let your mind drift forward to the present, stopping at any memory that comes to the surface.

Describe your parents' relationship. Think about the circumstances at the time of your birth, through childhood, adolescence, and early adulthood, to the present time. Consider the atmosphere of the household as generated by your parents' relationship. What secrets did they have from each other and from you?

W HEN YOU WERE growing up, you had a relationship or a lack of one with several significant relatives or caregivers. Each of those relationships informs who you are today.

Describe your relationships with each of your parents, siblings, and other relatives. If there were no siblings, write about significant family members (i.e., aunts, uncles, grandparents, godparents, cousins, etc.) or extended family. Think in terms of connection-disconnection, intimacy-independence, merging-separateness, friends-enemies, burden-joy, envy, jealousy, competition, support, concern, etc.

MUCH OF OUR IDENTITY is formed from the socio-economic-religious identifications of our family. One way to understand how you were imprinted by your family's circumstances is to imagine that they were different. Think of how different your life would be if your family had had more money, less money; imagine that you were born into a family with different religious beliefs or one from a different class. Visualize the neighborhood that you grew up in and think of the ways in which your home was like every other home in the neighborhood. Then remember the ways in which your home was different.

What was your family's socio-economic-religious background? What were the feelings in the household about the family situation? What were your feelings about it? What did this mean to the family and to you? How does this influence you in your life and relationships?

IN ORDER TO get into the spirit of the following question, take a few moments and imagine that you are at a family gathering. Remember what it is like when you greet one or both of your parents at the door, the feelings that are evoked. Now imagine that the family is sitting down to dinner, each in his or her place at the dinner table. The dinner conversation is coming back to you.

W hat was the family's style of communication, expression of feelings, affectional behavior (verbal affection and physical affection), discipline, fun, etc.?

The pain of love is the pain of being alive. It's a perpetual wound.

—MAUREEN DUFFY

FOR INFANTS, being loved is a very tangible experience. It is safety, food, warmth, being held and comforted. There is an innate longing for the feeling of being exquisitely attended to by the love object (in the case of childhood, the parent). Later, that longing gets transferred to siblings, peers, teachers, lovers, and friends. A trauma can be any moment, any situation where the world, especially the people in it, does not respond to you in the way you want or need at the time.

When I was six years old, I was on a television show with a group of other children. In the course of each program, Chucko the clown would make much fanfare over one lucky child's birthday. Though my birthday was just a few days away, another child was the focus of the birthday segment. I was devastated and couldn't understand why I had been overlooked. Evidently, even things that seem like small slights can have a lasting effect.

Take a few moments to revisit your childhood. Close your eyes, and as you breathe and relax allow yourself to drift back in time. Picture yourself on a magic carpet hovering above the memories. From this vantage point, you can see with some perspective. Stop and examine the times that were painful. See yourself at that age living through the events that were so difficult for you, your family, or other people you loved. Give yourself permission to remember all the feelings of those times. When you've captured the feelings, continue on to another memory. The magic carpet helps you maintain enough distance so that you are not caught up by the feelings but, rather, remain a compassionate witness.

List or describe any traumas or wounds that you remember. Big or small, hurt feelings, scary or sad moments, losses, humiliation, embarrassments—these are the wounds of childhood. Write about the feelings generated, in as much depth as is possible, paying particular attention to what these wounds mean to you.

No TWO FAMILIES are the same. You probably remember the family in your neighborhood in which every one of the children looked exactly alike. Some families are extremely close and tell one another everything. Other families are more a group of people who all live in the same boardinghouse; they share a place to sleep and a meal or two, but otherwise keep to themselves. Think about the ways in which you are very much a part of your family and can identify with the others. It is also necessary to reflect on the very important differences.

What similarities and
differences are there between
yourself and the other
members of your family?

The Philosopher

And what are you that, wanting you,
    I should be kept awake
As many nights as there are days
    With weeping for your sake?

And what are you that, missing you,
    As many days as crawl
I should be listening to the wind
    And looking at the wall?

I know a man that's a braver man
    And twenty men as kind,
And what are you, that you should be
    The one man in my mind?

Yet women's ways are witless ways,
    As any sage will tell,—
And what am I, that I should love
    So wisely and so well?

—Edna St. Vincent Millay

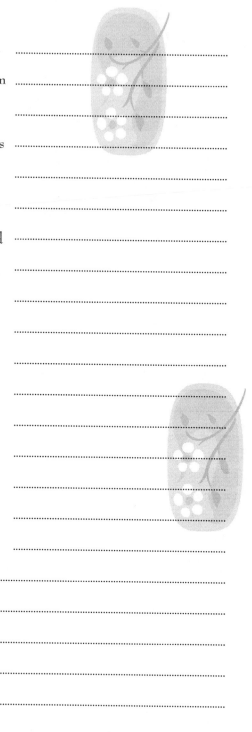

What themes or patterns have emerged from your relationships that remind you of your family's style? For example, your last partner was emotionally unavailable and rarely expressed affection toward you. Does this remind you of how you experienced a family member? How did your parents treat each other? Or, for instance, as a child you had the feeling that you couldn't get enough attention or your needs met. As a result, you learned how to take care of yourself and expect little from others. In your previous relationship, you noticed that your partner was quite self-absorbed and would operate out of convenience in relation to you—hence supporting your childhood belief that you couldn't expect much.

A child is the root of the heart.
—CAROLINA MARIA DE JESUS

EVERYTHING THAT EVER happened in your childhood lives inside you somewhere. Although you no longer consciously recall specific memories, your entire way of being is a living conversation constructed by what you felt happened to you as a child. Who you think you are, what you believe you can have or will never have, what you will become, the fears you have . . . all are directly connected to the intricate childhood formulation of self.

Robin, whose father separated many times from her mother and then finally moved out for good, believed that it would be difficult to find a steady, available man. Her father set the standard, and her mother insisted that most men were just the same. Lo and behold, Robin dated a series of men who were unable to commit to a relationship—a self-fulfilling prophecy built on belief systems that had been formed long ago.

TOUCH THE FEELING of endless longing. Never being important to somebody, never developing a relationship with your father, never feeling pretty, popular, and loved. Do you fantasize that your future partner will treat you or be with you unlike anything you've ever experienced with your family? Are you looking for the feeling that you could depend on someone else? Or perhaps that you never got information about how to develop, how to handle life situations, how to be a mature person. Do you ever say to yourself things like, "If I only had . . . the perfect mother"?

What was lost to you in childhood, what did you never have that you still want and are still looking for in your relationships?

....

....

....

....

....

....

....

....

....

....

....

....

....

....

....

....

....

....

....

....

THE FOLLOWING QUESTIONS address the ways in which you may be reexperiencing the mourning of a childhood loss. These old feelings attach themselves to current losses.

What past feelings or experiences have you been unable to get over that are coming up for you now in this state of grief? They could be from any part of your life. Are they connected?

Two-Volume Novel

The sun's gone dim, and
　　The moon's turned black;
For I loved him, and
　　He didn't love back.

—Dorothy Parker

THE FOLLOWING EXERCISE will clarify the congruity between the dynamics in your family of origin and the relationships you've created as an adult.

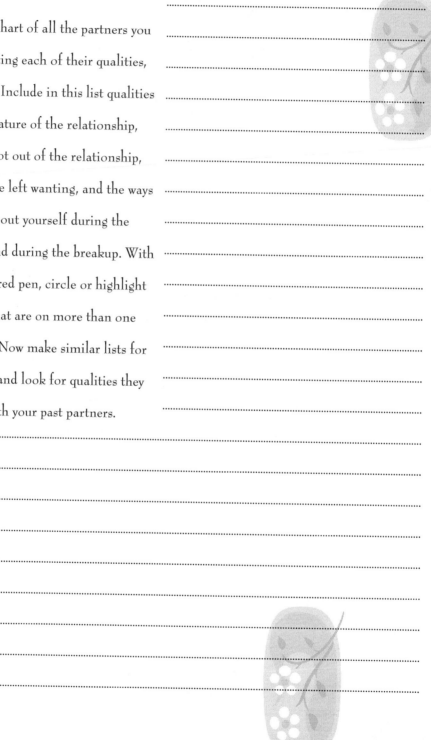

Make a chart of all the partners you have had, listing each of their qualities, good and bad. Include in this list qualities about the nature of the relationship, things you got out of the relationship, things you were left wanting, and the ways you felt about yourself during the relationship and during the breakup. With a bright-colored pen, circle or highlight the items that are on more than one partner's list. Now make similar lists for your parents and look for qualities they share with your past partners.

THESE QUESTIONS ARE particularly helpful for people who can't remember their childhood or the feelings in their home. By examining the patterns in your relationships, you will be able to reconstruct aspects of your childhood.

What themes or patterns have emerged in the types of romantic relationships you have been in? What similar feelings have shown up again? How are these patterns connected to your family?

....

....

....

....

....

....

....

....

....

....

....

....

....

....

....

....

....

....

....

The Minute I Heard My First Love Story

The minute I heard my first love story
I started looking for you, not knowing
How blind that was.

Lovers don't finally meet somewhere
They're in each other all along.

—Rumi

Partners may have very specific qualities that remind you of one or both of your parents—that is a direct connection to repetition compulsion. But more indirectly, a partner may bring up old familiar feelings we had toward our parents.

Old needs from childhood are harbored as deep longings. They appear as wishes that finally, "One day, someone will come along who will love me, see me, give to me what I never got." You think, "Maybe if I try hard enough or wait long enough, he/she will finally _____." And so you hold on, hoping that things will change.

In what ways did your ex-
partner resemble your
parents or engender feelings
you had as a child?

....
....
....
....
....
....
....
....
....
....

How have the similar-
ities between your ex and
your parents kept you from
letting go completely of
this past relationship?

....
....
....
....
....
....
....
....
....

Don't Let Your Throat Tighten

Don't let your throat tighten
with fear. Take sips of breath
all day and night, before death
closes your mouth.

—Rumi

I<small>T IS OFTEN</small> very difficult to give up obsessive thoughts about the old partner. No matter how useless it seems, these memories, questions, and thoughts haunt
for a long time. Most people, unless they have a very defended/rigid psyche, suffer
from this. Eventually, your mind will let these thoughts go.

What do you think will happen if you are no longer connected with this person, no longer thinking about this person?

EVEN THE BEST of friends might fail you at a particular moment when you're in need of support. Though heartbreak is nearly universal, they may have forgotten how it felt. They may not want to hear it anymore, or perhaps you yourself will tire of talking about what happened. Nevertheless, you still need to unburden yourself.

How does your best friend feel about your ex? If you could say anything to your best friend about your situation, what would that be? Have you already said everything you need to? If not—why not?

As you begin to heal from your broken heart, you are ready to think about future relationships. To select a more appropriate partner, let's learn from your past choices. The questions on the following page will help you to do that.

What kind of partner
are you attracted to? What
do you look for in a
partner?

What has worked for
you in past relationships?

In infatuation, the person is a *passive victim* of the spell of conceived attraction for the object. In love there is an *active appreciation* of the intrinsic worth of the object of love.

—MEHER BABA

KNOWING AND LOVING yourself are prerequisites to fully loving another. Instead of seeking a partner in an effort to be filled up, you will consciously choose an individual who you truly appreciate as a separate person. Most people are confused about the nature of self-love and how that translates to intimacy. When you have generosity of spirit, compassion, understanding, awareness, courage, resolve, and kindness directed toward yourself, you are filled with a very special kind of loving openness. You don't need anyone to give you this expansive feeling. Therefore, you can make a conscious and active appraisal of any partners who might come into your life.

After a breakup, especially if you feel rejected or responsible for what happened, you might be thinking that you have to lower your expectations. Perhaps you question whether you wanted and needed too much.

What do you believe
you should settle for in a
relationship?

T<small>AKE A FEW MOMENTS</small> and concentrate on acknowledging yourself; focus on your strengths and gifts. Think of at least ten things you appreciate about yourself and then answer the following questions. This is where the magic begins.

What do you believe
you are entitled to, deserve
to have, in a relationship?
What kind of relationship
are you looking for?

....

....

....

....

....

....

....

....

....

....

....

....

....

....

....

....

....

....

....

....

And the trouble is, if you don't risk anything, you risk even *more*.

—ERICA JONG

BEING HUMAN ENGENDERS in us the desire to love and be loved. When your heart has been broken, every old heartache in your body and spirit rises up and warns you to stay away from any potential love ache. The mere possibility of a rejection, even by someone you are barely attracted to, seems too threatening.

After staying in a long-distance relationship with a man for five years, Deborah gave her boyfriend an ultimatum. Not only did he refuse to marry her, but six months later she heard that he was engaged to another. That was ten long years ago, and although she is still a relatively young woman, she has refused to go out on a date ever since. Even as a child she thought that all she ever wanted was to marry and have children. Now, she can't even bring herself to create a possibility. Opening ourselves up again is a risk, but clearly the greater risk is to close ourselves off altogether.

RIGHT NOW you're still sore and aching from your broken heart. Human beings are designed to avoid pain and rarely regard it as essential to learning and growing. Don't listen to the part of your mind that tells you to avoid relationships because you've been hurt. In answering the following question, you can discover what kind of case you've been building to avoid being in a relationship.

W hat are your current fears about being in a relationship?

Keep Walking,
Though There's No Place to Get To

Keep walking, though there's no place to get to.

Don't try to see through the distances.

That's not for human beings. Move within,

but don't move the way fear makes you move.

—Rumi

JUST BEING WITH yourself—truly—is enough. There is nowhere to get to, nothing to succeed at, and nothing to change in this very moment. The precious minutes that we are able to fully inhabit are gifts of love and life. During difficult times, acts of self-care bring you back into a connection with your real life, not the life you once had, the one you wish you had, or the one you'll have someday. Breathe deliberately, take a long shower, call your best friend, clean out one drawer, drink a glass of water, walk, sing, file papers—these are all great steps.

What do you do to take care of yourself?

....

....

....

....

....

....

....

....

What are other things that you would like to do to take care of yourself?

....

....

....

....

....

....

....

....

OFTEN THERE are important tasks that you know would help you if you could/would just force yourself to do them . . . but it just doesn't happen. After you lose a relationship, the familiar weekly routine has disappeared. When you create a regular habit of positive self-care, you inadvertently establish a self-sustaining structure. Think about this as you respond to the following questions.

What self-care activities are difficult for you right now?

....

....

....

....

....

....

....

....

....

What might you commit to doing every week that is just for you?

....

....

....

....

....

....

....

....

....

Healed

Oh, when I flung my heart away,
  The year was at its fall.
I saw my dear, the other day,
  Beside a flowering wall;
And this was all I had to say:
  "I thought that he was tall!"

—Dorothy Parker

An AFFIRMATION IS a positive statement that expresses the best possible description of feelings, situations, and outcomes. For example, "I am a beautiful person, full of love. I am free to give and receive love." Or, "All of life's experiences have contributed in magical ways to the wonderful, loving partner I am."

Write out ten affirmations stating that you are (present tense) healing, that your life is good, that everything is meaningful and transformative, that you are lovable, that you will love again, that you will pass through this experience in an amazing way, etc.

Married

I came back from the funeral and crawled
around the apartment, crying hard,
searching for my wife's hair.
For two months got them from the drain,
from the vacuum cleaner, under the refrigerator,
and off the clothes in the closet.
But after other Japanese women came,
there was no way to be sure which were
hers, and I stopped. A year later,
repotting Michiko's avocado, I find
a long black hair tangled in the dirt.

—Jack Gilbert

IT MAY SEEM repetitive to keep saying good-bye, but you know better than anyone how much or how often thoughts and feelings for your ex still haunt you. It is useful to continue to encourage yourself in this gentle way.

Write another good-bye letter to the relationship and the loved one. Include what you plan to do to take care of yourself (loving and healthy commitments to yourself in the future). Make this a complete and thorough good-bye. End with three affirmations about self-love, deserving love, and how good it feels to let go.

It's EASY TO THINK of the things you miss from your last relationship and imagine having those good qualities in your next relationship. It's also important to be clear about the parts of prior relationships that you never want to go through again.

What did you learn
from this experience that
you would want to avoid in
future relationships?

Body, Remember . . .

Body, remember not only how much you were loved,

not only the beds you lay on,

but also those desires that glowed openly

in eyes that looked at you,

trembled for you in the voices—

only some chance obstacle frustrated them.

Now that it's all finally in the past,

it seems almost as if you gave yourself

to those desires too—how they glowed,

remember, in eyes that looked at you,

remember, body, how they trembled for you in those voices.

—Constantine Cavafy,

 translated by Edmund Keeley and Phillip Sherrard

Full-out mourning is a valuable learning process. It has deepened your capacity to feel, opened your heart to a greater depth of compassion, and enhanced your wisdom about the purpose or meaning of life's changes.

If you have children or imagine speaking to a child, what would you explain to them about the purpose and the value of change, loss, and grief?

Everyday happiness means getting up in the morning, and you can't wait to finish your breakfast. You can't wait to do your exercises. You can't wait to put on your clothes. You can't wait to get out—and you can't wait to come home, because the soup is hot.

—GEORGE BURNS

FULLY MOURNING a loss leads to the conclusion that life is good. When your heart was broken, you could not conceive of a day that would come when you would be at peace. For a while the everyday tasks of life felt unbearable; now these same activities are the gentle structure of the life you are creating for yourself. Knowing that you can come through a loss and feel stronger and healthier gives you the courage to take greater risks. Rather than avoiding life, now is the time to devour it, in the full knowledge that there is a cycle of growth, flowering, dying, and rebirth to every relationship.

A Walk

My eyes already touch the sunny hill,
going far ahead of the road I have begun.
So we are grasped by what we cannot grasp;
it has its inner light, even from a distance—

and changes us, even if we do not reach it,
into something else, which, hardly sensing it, we already are;
a gesture waves us on, answering our own wave . . .
but what we feel is the wind in our faces.

—Rainer Maria Rilke

Visualize yourself free of grief. Give thanks for this experience, give thanks for letting go, pray, sing, and repeat your affirmations.

Describe a full picture
of where you would like to
be in your life and what
you would like to be doing
a year from now.

Spring Ceremony

IT IS TIME to clear the way for new things. The first step is sorting through the contents of your home. Empty out your drawers, your closets, and your counters of all the clutter. Be ruthless. Anything that ties you to the pain of the past should be tossed. Get rid of anything that makes you feel bad about yourself. Then, clean your place from top to bottom. Go to the flower shop and bring home a bouquet. If you have a garden, buy plants to symbolize the new growth you anticipate.

Create an altar, and fill it with items that symbolize all the changes that are coming—the love you expect to enter your life. Perhaps you want to include red roses for passion or a ring to represent commitment and wholeness. Every time you pass your altar, stop for a moment and give thanks for the riches in your life, the love that is already available, the little things that give you joy, and the wisdom that you've gathered by working through this guide.

We've been on a long journey together. You've completed an important and arduous piece of work. Not everyone has the temerity you have demonstrated. You've looked deeply at your childhood, the origin of your pain, and learned how those early influences have shaped the relationships you've had as an adult. You've walked through the memories that contributed to the loss of this relationship. And you've taken the time for yourself. It's time to congratulate yourself, to reflect on all the ways you've grown and acknowledge all you've learned.

What have you
learned? About yourself?
About grief? About life?

....
....
....
....
....
....
....
....
....
....
....
....
....
....
....
....
....
....
....
....
....
....

Since everything is but an apparition, perfect in being what it is, having nothing to do with good or bad, acceptance or rejection, one may well burst out in laughter.

—LONGCHENPA

Permissions

Notes

Notes